THIS BOOK CAN BE AN INSPIRATION TO KIDS AND ADULTS WHO DARE TO **DREAM BIG**

Whenever you see a QR code like the one below, scan using your phone camera to follow the adventure of Clovis Salmon as he receives his O.B.E. at Windsor Castle.

CLOVIS SALMON GOES TO
Windsor Castle

Published by L.O. Publishing

Editor Donald Hammond &
Anísa Thomas

Copyright © [2024] by [Liára Oladele]

All rights reserved.

No portion of this book may be reproduced in any form without written permission from the publisher or author, except as permitted by U.S. copyright law.

INVESTITURE
AT
WINDSOR CASTLE

One day as I sat and opened my mail,
I saw advertisements, offers, and even must-have sales.
But then I saw something that really caught my eye.
A letter from the King of England! What a lovely surprise!
Wow, why would King Charles III be writing to me?
Oh my, oh my, what could it be!

The King of England has nominated me,
Yes, me to receive an O.B.E.!

The letter stated I needed to accept the honor from the King, before His Majesty could proceed to do anything.

After that, they would post the honor in the London Gazette, And then I would know just what to do next.

The London Gazette posted it online!
This is great news, I didn't even have to wait a long time.

THE GAZETTE
OFFICIAL PUBLIC RECORD

Published by Authority | Est 1665

All Awards and Accreditation notices | WW1 notices | WW1 medals | Resources

Notice details

Type:
State
> Order of the British Empire

Publication date:
29 December 2023, 22:39

Edition:
The London Gazette

Issue number:
64269

Notice ID:
4520386

Notice code:
1129

Order of the British Empire

Civil Division

Central Chancery of the Orders of Knighthood

St. James's Palace, London SW1

30 December 2023

THE KING has been graciously pleased to give orders for the following promotions in, and appointments to, the Most Excellent Order of the British Empire:

O.B.E.

To be Ordinary Officers of the Civil Division of the said Most Excellent Order:

Clovis Constantine SALMON

Documentary Filmmaker

For services to Culture and to the Black Community.

Actions

- Order as a commemorative product
- Save notice to My Gazette
- Download PDF of this issue
- Print notice
- Share this notice
- Linked data view
- Provenance trail

Digital Signature

- Signed Document HTML
- Signature for HTML Document
- Signed RDF Document
- Signed Provenance RDF
- What is a digital signature?

The post said I had been appointed to receive the Most Excellent Order of the British Empire (O.B.E.).
Oh my goodness, I could not believe I would receive such a thing!
I wonder what else the day will bring!

The post further explained that I had been chosen to receive the honor for my Services to Culture and the Black Community as a documentary filmmaker.

It is truly a blessing to be recognized for my talent as a wheel builder, and now by the King of England for my talent as a filmmaker.

Shortly after, I received the Honor letter.
Then, a second one arrived. Wow, how can this get any better?

This is so exciting, I should probably put on the kettle.
I was told I would receive my Investiture at Windsor Castle
and that I should choose only three guests to go with me.
Oh my, oh my, who would the other three be?

Mrs. Salmon will be pleased to go with me.
Oh my, oh my, who will the other two be?
I know, it should be my two daughters, Sandra and Valerie!
When I asked them, they said they would be honored to go with me.

So, I responded to the Honor Letter and said, "I know, I know who will be going with me.

It will be

Mrs. Salmon, Sandra and Valerie."

Wait! When I go to see the King, what will we wear?
Oh, wait, on the invitation, it says it right there.

We'll all wear traditional Morning and Day Dress,
so honestly, there's really no need for us to stress.

What would you wear? Write below

_____
_____
_____
_____
_____
_____
_____

I waited and waited, and one day, my invitation came in the mail. Three tickets for Windsor Castle. One, two, three. Can you count with me?

1

2

3

and one for me

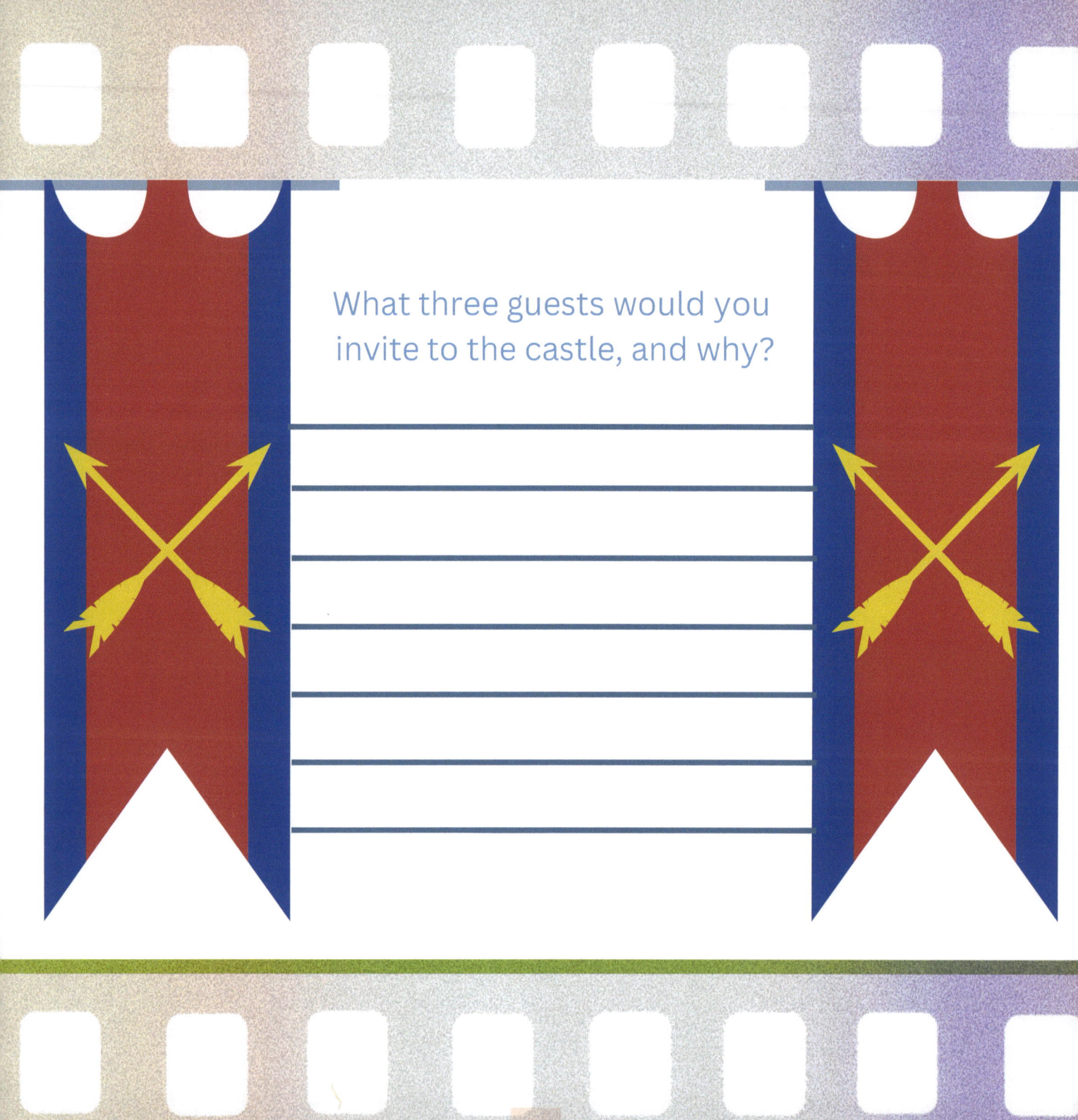

What three guests would you invite to the castle, and why?

Now, it's time for Mrs. Salmon and me
to lay out the clothes for the Investiture Ceremony.

Mrs. Salmon found the dress she would wear to the ceremony.
It is as blue as the sky, and boy, it is pretty!

My grandson Shaun is buying my suit for me.
He took me to Hawes and Curtis, which one will be right for me?

The store attendant and my grandson did a great job indeed.
I left with a suit and shoes that were just right for me.

Windsor Castle is far away from Brixton.
I needed a hotel, and my daughter helped me pick one.
She found a hotel just a short distance from Windsor.
We were all very grateful for that, to be sure.

It was time, so my family and I made our way to the hotel.
There is so much to do we can't even sit down and watch the news,
or take a snooze.

I have to lay out my outfit, including my socks, shoes and hat.
They need to be perfect before I can hit the mat.

I can see Windsor Castle from the hotel window.
The castle lights up at night, and it is so beautiful!
I can't wait—I can't wait until tomorrow.
I know many others will be there receiving awards and saying bravo!

It's time to say goodnight and get some rest;
I don't want to stay up all night and then have to stress.
I know that tomorrow will be the best!
That is why now I have to get some rest.

It's morning! Time to get up, no time to wait.
I've got to get dressed because I don't want to be late.

Oh my goodness, just look at the time.
I can't believe how quickly time has flown by!

Knock, knock, knock. I hear a knock at the door.
Who can it be knocking at my door?
Oh look, oh look, it is my family!
They came to my room to meet up with me!
But wait, is there time to sit down and have some tea?

Oh no, oh no, it is time to go.
Let's quickly take a few pictures before we go.

We're all set, It's time to head to the car.
It will be a short walk because the car is not very far.
I'm so excited; there is no time to wait.
Off I go, I've got a very important date.
No time to waste, no time to waste,
or else we will be terribly late.

My family and I were swift and made our way to the lift, down to the lobby, out of the hotel, and began walking to the car park. Boy, was it a long walk.

There are many lovely shops along the way,
and I really would like to stay,
but I will have to wait until later on today.
There is a DonutTime, a boutique, and a Build-a-Bear shop.
There are so many nice stores, but we don't have time to stop.

Mrs. Salmon, Sandra, Valerie, and I
entered into our car.
To drive to Windsor Castle,
which was not very far.
I can't wait! I can't wait!
I don't want to be late!

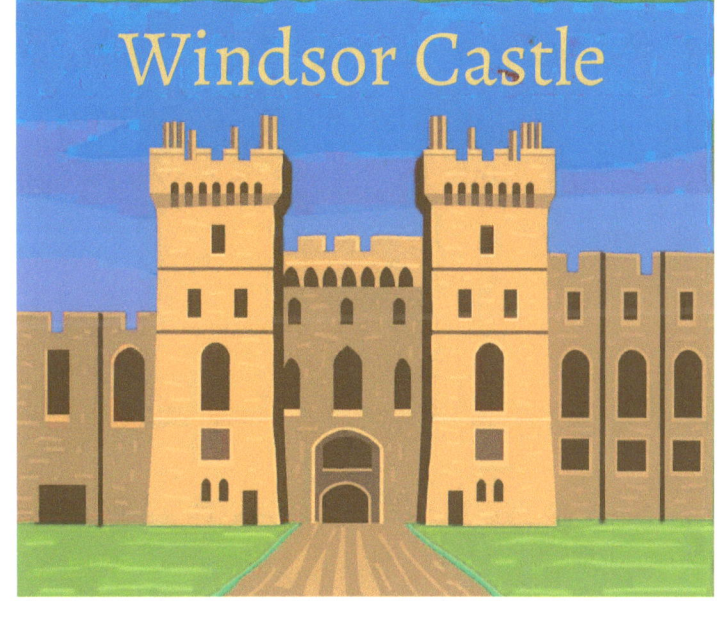

Which way would you take? Scan the QR code to follow my family on their adventure to Windsor Castle.

We finally arrived at the Windsor Castle gate. Hello, here are our tickets.
I was nominated by the King to receive an O.B.E.
And I am so glad to have my family with me!

We finally arrived at the entrance of the castle,
and we were escorted down the hallway without any hassle.
Along the walls, there were large portraits of Kings and Queens.
Oh my goodness, what a lovely scene!

They took us to a large room, where I had to
wait for my name to be called.
I thanked the Lord and almost bawled.

"Mr. Clovis Salmon for Services to Culture
and the Black Community",
they announced.
Wow, I can't believe they called me.
So many others were there watching me
and waiting to receive their honor, just like me!

I was escorted in front of Princess Royal.

"You're the one who filmed the Brixton Riot. It was very good," she said.

She also mentioned that
she liked what I did,
and that it was great work!
Then she reached out her hand and firmly shook mine!
Boy, I am having such a lovely time!

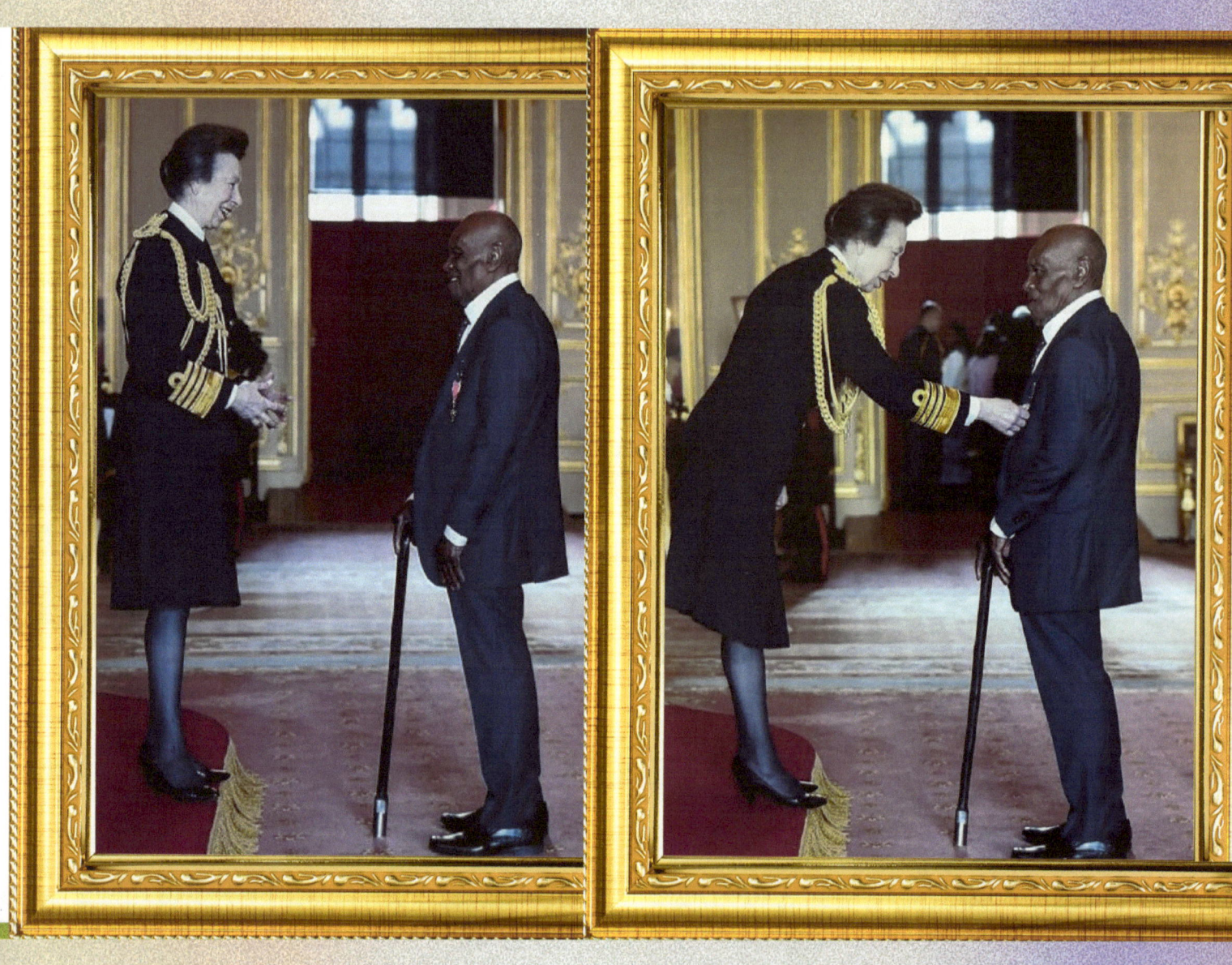

After I received my O.B.E. I had a very special picture taken of me.

Soon, I will have that picture on my bookshelf. Do you have a special picture of someone or yourself?

Mrs. Salmon, Sandra, and I were escorted back to our car.
Where we met with the rest of our family,
that were waiting outside the castle for me.

Today was such a blessed day,
and I thank Jesus for everything he has done to get me through the day!

Blessed Day!
Do not give up on your dreams! Dream

CHECK OUT THE WEBSITE BELOW TO LEARN MORE ABOUT PLACES TO VISIT & STAY AROUND WINDSOR CASTLE

1. VISIT WINDSOR CASTLE HTTPS://WWW.RCT.UK/VISIT/WINDSOR-CASTLE/TOP-THINGS-TO-SEE-AND-DO-AT-WINDSOR-CASTLE

2. VISIT THE SHOPPING CENTER AROUND WINDSOR CASTLE HTTPS://WINDSORROYAL.CO.UK/

Dream BIG!

What dream(s) do you want to achieve?

What can I do to try to reach for my dream(s):

Why is this dream important to me:

What problems might get in the way of me trying to reach my goal, and how will I overcome them:

How long will it take me to reach my goal:

When I feel like giving up, I will tell myself...

DREAM BIG!

DRAW, COLOR, GLUE OR PASTE YOUR DREAM GOAL BELOW.

I invite you to submit an essay explaining your dream and the steps that you will take to reach it.

Win a free signed copy of "Clovis Salmon Goes to Windsor Castle.

- One free copy will be given away each month, along with a London souvenir.
- Open to all ages.
- Answer the question, "What is your dream job and how do you plan to do to achieve it? (350 words or less).

Send essay to liara@liarasroyaltearoom.com
Accepted file types: Microsoft Word, PDF or JPEG.

Bibliography

Authority,The Gazette Official Public Record." Accessed August 20, 2024. The Gazette https://www.thegazette.co.uk/.

The Stationary Office, "Order British Empire Notice," Accessed August 20, 2024. The Gazette https://www.thegazette.co.uk/notice/4520386.

Eagleton, Justin, *Windsor Map,* 2018, Windsor Central Travelodge, United Kingdom.

www.ingramcontent.com/pod-product-compliance
Lightning Source LLC
Chambersburg PA
CBHW042003150426
43194CB00002B/110